My Poetic Thoughts in Life
Reflection of Civil Rights & The Holy Spirit

Jason E. White

ISBN: 979-8-9869701-1-0

www.tfieldinglowecompany.com

DEDICATION

To God, who is the head of my life, I thank you for putting in me what I can give to the world.

To my father Ernest, a.k.a. "Pappy," and my aunt Anna, I love and miss you both, and soon we'll reunite with you in Heaven.

To my momma, Sandra, thank you for raising me to be a strong, confident young man, and lastly, to all my ancestors from slavery, your legacy shall never be forgotten.

INTRODUCTION

When I was younger, my momma said something that stuck with me for years. She said, "Son, the people on television are no different from you. The only difference is that they tapped into their talents. You got to find yours".

In my teens and 20s, I spent more time watching other talents and less time working on my own, mostly because I didn't know what my talent was within me. At first, I wanted to be a sports reporter, but the problem was you had to ask some personal questions. A perfect example was Ray Lewis, an NFL player who was acquitted of murder in 2000. One year later, he led the Baltimore Ravens to the Super Bowl, but the media asked Lewis about his murder trial instead of asking about the game. That's where I knew that reporting wasn't for me. I'd even wanted to be a radio disc jockey, but my interest in that quickly faded.

It wasn't until my late 30's that I discovered poetry and spoken words as my calling in life. As an African American, it was critical to address black issues. My momma reminded me of how I would grow up as a black man, and the police would try to stop me for no reason. She could not be more right, especially when I heard about George Floyd, Tamir Rice, Michael Brown, Breonna Taylor, Sandra Bland, and Eric Garner being killed by the police.

This makes me meditate on Psalms 37:23. The Bible says, "The Lord orders the steps of a good man; I believe that Floyd, Aubery, and others were good, ambitious people, and they were just in the wrong place at the wrong time. So as I go out for my daily routine, I ask the Lord to guide my steps so I won't suffer the same fate. In addition it was important to honor leaders like Harriet Tubman, Frederick Douglass, Dr. Martin Luther King Jr., Rosa Parks and Jackie Robinson. Without their sacrifice Black America wouldn't have the opportunities they have today.

I have a sense of calling to write about God and the issues of life. God has put it in my heart to ask questions that no preacher, evangelist, or anyone thought of asking. My purpose is to inspire generations to fight for peace, freedom, justice, and righteousness for our Lord and Savior, Jesus. God bless you.

-January 2022

TABLE OF CONTENTS

*

SOMEWHERE ON MY MIND

We are living in a nation full of hate crimes, police brutalities, and racial injustice. When I look at what's happening in America, somewhere on my mind, I think about Marvin Gaye asking, "What's Going On?" or Curtis Mayfield sang, "Don't Worry," or James Brown saying it loud, "I'm Black, and I'm Proud."

Then somewhere on my mind, I thought about that "Rumble young man rumble," you know, that young fighter who was told to fight the Vietnam War. When he refused, he was stripped of his heavyweight title and served three years in prison. But his message was clear, why fight a nation that doesn't hate, discriminate and segregate as America does?

Then somewhere on my mind, I thought about that civil rights leader who dreamed of a diverse and equal nation. Forty-five years later, a brotha' from Chicago became that dream when he was elected as the 44th President of the United States.

Now I wanted to stop thinking, but when I look at the senseless killings of Trayvon Martin, Michael Brown, Eric Garner, Ahmaud Aubery, Breonna Taylor, and George Floyd somewhere, I think about that 14-year-old boy who was killed in Mississippi in 1955. Like this 14-year-old, neither victim got justice, and their killers have walked free.

Added insult to injury, far too many times I've seen young black men being arrested, charged, and convicted of a crime they never committed. When that happened, I thought about "To Kill A Mockingbird" from 1962. In that film, a black man was falsely accused of raping a white woman. Though there was no evidence against him, the defendant was found guilty not of rape but his race.

We're dealing with police who want to kill and neglect rather than serve and protect. To those officers, I would ask you this question, if you were to die today, what would Jesus say? "Well done thy good and faithful servant" or "Depart from me, I never knew you." If only we thought about that question, then we all would spend time with God, repent of our sins and give our lives to Christ. Once we do, somewhere in our minds, we'll be like that civil rights leader saying, "Free at last, free at last, by the grace of God, we are free at last."

WE ARE STILL ENSLAVED

Four centuries ago, we were brought here to America by a group of slave owners. Former slaves like Harriet Tubman, Frederick Douglass, and Sojourner Truth have worked hard to end slavery, but despite their efforts, I'm sad to say that four centuries later, we are still enslaved.

Enslaved by police officers who have pulled us over, interrogated, and shot us to death. Enslaved by being the first to be fired and the last to be hired. Enslaved by TV that shows, ballers, rappers, and gangstas; not doctors, lawyers, and leaders.

Worst of all, we're still enslaved by a nation that hates, discriminates, and segregates. It's no wonder why freedom doesn't mean we are free; when being enslaved mentally and psychologically. I pray that someday we will no longer be enslaved and, for once, be encouraged.

HE TOOK A KNEE

In 2016, an NFL quarterback refused to stand during the national anthem. When asked why? His message was clear. There is too much racism, brutality, and injustice against African Americans. Of course, America refused to listen, but that changed when George Floyd was murdered. That is why HE TOOK A KNEE.

He took a knee so that we could take a STAND, a stand for freedom, justice, and equality for all Americans.

He took a knee so we could take a LOOK, a look at how we need to change not only as Americans but as God's people.

He took a knee so that we could take a MOMENT, a moment to honor Dr. King, Rosa Parks, and all the leaders of civil rights.

More importantly, he took a knee so we can take the TIME, a time to turn our voices into action.

To Colin Kaepernick, thank you for taking a knee, for if you hadn't taken a knee, we would never fight to be free.

MORE THAN A FIST

In 1968 two sprinters raised their fists to honor Black America, but if you understood why they did it, then you would agree that Tommie Smith and John Carlos raised more than just a fist.

They also raised a generation that will fight against discrimination.

They also raised a freedom cry to show no negro has to die.

They raised a message very clear that we as blacks should never fear.

They raised demands to set us free like Kaepernick when he took a knee, and they raised a call to fight for peace against the threats of the so-called police.

What started as a negro fist is now a fight that still exists.

NO JUSTICE!! NO PEACE!!

BLACK ACTS MATTER

As Black America, we're blessed with films like Malcolm X, Roots, and The Black Panther. These films are living proof that black ACTS matter.

Negro acts that represent what being black has truly meant.

Negro acts that reprimand a Hollywood that shouldn't stand.

Negro acts that reached the goal of giving blacks a major role.

Negro acts with a role to play in allowing blacks to have their say, and negro acts with a tone to set in making films we won't forget.

The negro films that have been seen left a legacy on the movie screen.

BLACK DREAMS MATTER

After George Floyd's death, the black community came out with a message that black lives matter. One of the ways to prove it is by reminding America that black DREAMS matter.

Negro dreams of a little child who's gonna struggle for a while.

Negro dreams of a teenager with no risk being in danger.

Negro dreams bring unity like Dr. King's back in '63.

Negro dreams of no more pain but love and peace beyond Soul Train, and negro dreams of a U.S.A. where all the blacks will have their say.

Once that occurs, our negro goals will get us out of these racial holes.

BLACK MINDS MATTER

After George Floyd's murder, our generation sent a clear message that black lives matter, but there was a time in the last four centuries where black MINDS matter and they still matter even today.

Negro minds like Dr. King, who once declared, "Let freedom ring."

Negro minds like Malcolm X who set the tone for who's coming next.

Negro minds like Harriet who freed the slaves she wouldn't forget.

Negro minds like Douglass who saved the slaves from brutal stress.

Negro minds like Rosa Parks whose sacrifice left future marks, and negro minds like the champ Ali, who floated and stung like a fighting bee.

Though the negro minds are earthly dead, they paved the way for black lives ahead.

BLACK QUEENS MATTER

What do Breonna Taylor and Sandra Bland have in common? They were among the young black sistas killed by the police. To prevent this from happening, we must protect our sistas' and declare that black QUEENS matter.

All the queens from the motherland like Rosa Parks, refused to stand.

All the queens being on the run to raise a daughter and save her son.

All the queens with no drama like the beautiful Michelle Obama.

All the queens who are deep within are beautiful with their brown skin, and all the queens who deserve a crown for letting nobody tear them down.

We want to tell our negro queens to keep striving by any means.

BLACK SOUNDS MATTER

After George Floyd's murder, the whole Black America came out and declared that black lives matter. More than a movement, it's a reflection of how black SOUNDS matter, especially in music.

Negro sounds like Marvin Gaye asked what's going on in the U.S.A.

Negro sounds like Holiday singing "Strange Fruit," as Billie may.

Negro sounds like James Brown who would say it loud and break it down.

Negro sounds like the Queen of Soul who commands respect or will shut your hole, and negro sounds that will rejoice if we learn to sing and lift every voice.

Until we ring with harmony, we must sing the songs of liberty.

BLACK STORIES MATTER

The senseless murder of George Floyd started a movement that said "Black Lives Matter". What is just a slogan to America that has been living proof that black STORIES matter?

Negro stories with the victory from evil minds of slavery.

Negro stories with a common dream of this nation working as a team.

Negro stories with the civil rights that will put an end to all racial fights.

Negro stories with a firm demand that racism just cannot stand, and negro stories with a voice to use for all the blacks who's been abused.

Let the negro stories inspire you to change the whole red, white and blue.

BLACK VOICES MATTER

The death of George Floyd pushed African Americans to speak up and declare that black lives matter. Among those blacks were athletes who have proven over the years how black VOICES matter both in and outside of sports.

Negro voices with every scar like the great Kareem Abdul-Jabbar.

Negro voices from town to town who battled race like Jim Brown.

Negro voices fighting every day like the champ who used to be Cassius Clay.

Negro voices like 42 of the Brooklyn Dodgers, just a name a few.

Negro voices who had to clash like the one in tennis named Arthur Ashe, and black voices like LeBron James, who spoke up and dribbled in all his games.

The legacies are signed and sealed for these black voices outside the field.

BLACK YOUTHS MATTER

What do Trayvon Martin, Michael Brown, Tamir Rice, Ahmaud Aubery, and Breonna Taylor have in common?

They were all young, innocent black people killed for no reason besides their race. That's why we must say that not only black lives matter but black YOUTHS matter.

Negro youths who go to school for education are their only tool.

Negro youths who want to learn the same respect that their parents earn.

Negro youths who want to see how they can get a college degree.

Negro youths who can do so good in living lives outside the hood, and negro youths who will spend a day igniting the dream of Dr. MLK.

That dream will come when we have the will to prevent a future Emmett Till.

LET MY BROTHAS' GO

Through Moses, God said to Pharaoh, "Let my people go." There are many Pharaohs in law enforcement, and as a black man, I'm telling the police to let my BROTHAS' go.

Let my brothas' go-ahead to a family that must be led.

Let my brothas' go along when there's no proof of doing wrong.

Let my brothas' go to class for every test they need to pass.

Let my brothas' go on back without another police attack. And let my brothas' grow to be the men their sons would want to see.

My brothas' have a lot to show if the police learn to let them go.

A BIRTH QUAKE

To be born again is to repent and give your life to Jesus. When that happens, Hell feels an earthquake, and Heaven feels a BIRTH quake.

A birthing quake that celebrates those who repent in all the states.

A birthing quake that spread the news that those in Christ shall never lose.

A birthing quake that breaks the walls and sets you free of Satan's jaws.

A birthing quake that makes you feel like you and God have made a deal, and a birthing quake that's gonna claim that everyone won't be the same.

Knowing Christ is the step to take to give Heaven a major BIRTH quake.

A CONTRACT EXTENSION

In sports, players and coaches agree to a contract extension to stay with their teams. As a believer, you should do the same with God through a CONTACT extension.

Extend your time with his holy word so you'll spread the good news that must be heard.

Extend your time using every thought about all the lessons the Lord has taught.

Extend your time to speak with Christ with the faith to know he'll be precise.

Extend the talk you had before about trusting God in doing more, and extend the talk you're having now with a God who knows just when and how.

It's only God you must depend for a contact that you can extend.

A CONVERSATION WITHIN

A conversation is one of the most important acts in life, especially with the person used to be. When you look back over your life, every now and then, you should spend time with yourself and have a conversation within.

A conversation with that little child that you used to be just acting wild.

A conversation with an inner teen who was rebellious and flat-out mean.

A conversation with a younger you refusing what you were told to do.

A conversation with lessons to share with you who did wrong and didn't care, and a conversation that will inspire your future self to have God's desire. That godly desire will help you win if you only speak to that person.

A DEAD MAN STALKING

In the Bible Satan like a roaring lion sought whom he could devour. As a believer, you need God's protection, for Satan is a dead man STALKING.

A dead man stalking on you and me 'cause the God we serve had set us free.

A dead man stalking any man who will follow Christ the best he can.

A dead man stalking families who pray to God on bended knees.

A dead man stalking humankind who needs the Lord when it is blind, and a dead man stalking on each of us who will always have our father's trust?

By trusting God, you'll take a walk on the enemy who tries to stalk you.

GET YOUR KNEES OFF OUR NECKS

On behalf of our slain negroes, we're telling America to get your KNEES off our NECKS.

Now get those knees of slavery off of negroes fighting to be free.

Just get those knees of the police force off of blacks whose God is the only source.

Just get those knees of the Ku Klux Klan off of the innocence of a negro man.

Just get those knees from the Jim Crow off of young negroes who want to grow, and get those knees that lynched for years off of all black folks with silent tears.

America will stay a wreck with its' knees leaning on a negro's neck.

NO JUSTICE NO PEACE!!

WE ARE STILL GETTING LYNCHED

For decades, our negroes got lynched for their race. Although the times have changed, racism hasn't. 'Cause we are still getting LYNCHED.

We're still getting lynched for being black by the way America held us back.

We're still getting lynched for being here demanding justice every year.

We're still getting lynched for being proud like James Brown singing "Say it loud".

We're still getting lynched for being right in protesting each day and night, and we're still getting lynched for being mad at cops who treat us very bad.

We, as blacks, must take the inch to save ourselves from another lynch.

NO JUSTICE, NO PEACE!!

A DEFENSIVE FRIEND

In football, a defensive end tackles and sacks quarterbacks. In Heaven, a defensive FRIEND tackles and sacks the enemy.

A defensive friend who stripped the ball from the pits of Hell when he took the fall. A defensive friend who'll intimidate a society who wants to hate. A defensive friend who'll find the space to help you run this Christian race.

A defensive friend whose only job is to take down the Devil's mob and a defensive friend you want to seek if you gonna win every single week. Jesus is my defensive FRIEND with miracles he's gonna send. Peace out!!

NOT ALL BLACKS ARE GHETTO

Each day African Americans are viewed as thugs and animals. As a proud negro I'm serving notice that not all blacks are GHETTO.

Not all negroes in the U.S.A. are causing trouble every day.

Not all negroes in this "Freedom" land have a gun or knife in every hand.

Not all negroes are there to hang with everyone who's in a gang.

Not all negroes are there to fight or do hip hop each day and night, nor all negroes are there to play to make money in the NBA. There are negroes who want to make a huge difference for Heaven's sake.

A FALL FOR YOUR WALL

In the Bible, Joshua walked around the walls of Jericho, the people shouted and the walls came tumbling down. Like Joshua, you, too, can walk around and see a FALL for your wall.

A type of fall for every doubt that's keeping you from the Lord's route.

A type of fall for every curse that the pits of Hell try to rehearse.

A type of fall for every man who does not hold the father's hand.

A type of fall with a clearer view of fallen walls in front of you and a type of fall with a victory over every wall of the enemy.

Your Jericho will take the fall if you follow God, who does it all.

A FALSE HEART

In football, a player gets penalized for a false start. Come judgment day; this world will be penalized for a false HEART.

A false heart keeps you in a darker place where you'll never win. A false heart keeps you down, and you'll never get your holy crown. A false heart puts you through a life that makes you sad and blue.

A false heart blocks your face from seeing God through a higher place, and a false heart will always be the reason why you can't be free. If you want to get a newer start you must throw away that lying heart. Peace out!!

A GUILE BEHIND A SMILE

Back in the 70s, there was a song where smiling faces sometimes didn't tell the truth. Over the years, the song became a reality because, in some people, there's a guile behind a smile.

A type of smile that has deceit and is looking for those it can defeat. A type of smile that tells a lie and doesn't care who has to die. A type of smile that is full of hate to a point it wants to manipulate.

A type of smile that will make you sick by using the Devil's dirty trick, and a type of smile that looks to kill and gives someone a demonic thrill. So don't be fooled by every smile in the world, full of lust and guile. God bless y'all.

A HOUSE IS NEVER A HOME

In the Bible, Jesus said he was standing at the door knocking, and if anyone opened, he would spend time with them during dinner. You may live in a nice house, a big mansion, or an apartment, but without Jesus Christ, a house is never a home.

It ain't a home when a tragedy is tearing apart the whole family.

It ain't a home when one adult living with another is difficult.

It ain't a home when you suffer stress 'cause life became a total mess.

It ain't a home for parenthood when your own children ain't doing good, and it ain't a home for anyone without the Lord's begotten son.

Let Jesus Christ be your resident, and you'll have the peace that he has sent.

A HOUSE TRAP

The Bible described Hell as the lake of fire, it's the last place you want to go 'cause Hell is a HOUSE trap.

It's a house trap of the enemy that burns you up eternally.

It's a house trap from the pits of Hell, and going there won't do you well.

It's a house trap for all the souls who put themselves in Satan's holes.

It's a house trap for every folk who robs and kills with the Devil's stroke, and a house trap you won't escape for your sins that got you out of shape.

So take a seat on your father's lap, and you'll avoid a hellish trap.

A LAND WITHOUT TIME

When I was younger, there was a film called A Land Before Time where only dinosaurs existed. When I die, I want to go to a land WITHOUT time where only believers existed.

A land without a running clock 'cause it's only ruled by the solid rock.

A land without a sound alarm 'cause it's filled with love and tender charm.

A land without a watch to wear for a time of praise is always there.

A land without a single take on how much time did Jesus make, and a land without a single view of when Jesus welcomes you.

Heaven will never pass its prime 'cause it serves a God that needs no time.

A LEGAL WEAPON

Somewhere in the Bible, our weapons are not carnal but strong and mighty in God. No matter what battles you must face, you have a legal weapon to use in the word of God.

A legal weapon that is good enough to tackle life when it's getting rough.

A legal weapon that has the might to defeat your giants in every fight.

A legal weapon that has the tools to defeat a world full of hating fools.

A legal weapon that you'll only want against an enemy who is on a hunt, and a legal weapon that's gonna last and wash away your sinful past.

While the enemy has his killing sword, you got a legal weapon that's from the Lord.

A LIFE BEYOND

Somewhere in the Bible, Jesus came to give us life and that more abundantly. If I were to translate, I would say that Jesus wants to give us life beyond normal.

A life beyond a daily routine that, chances are, doesn't mean a thing.

A life beyond just going to work with a group of folks who are just berserk.

A life beyond what you really see in our world today externally.

A life beyond just what you hear from the worldly voices that are drawing fear, and a life beyond these present days that God has promised in biblical ways.

Just put yourself in Jesus' from experiencing life beyond the norm.

A LIFE UNBROKEN

Many years ago, there was an old saying, "If it ain't broke, don't try to fix it." That is what God stands for by giving you a life unbroken.

A kind of life with no repairs when serving God who really cares.

A kind of life without any tools when serving God and his holy rules.

A kind of life that doesn't crack when knowing God really has your back.

A kind of life that doesn't fall when the God you serve breaks every wall, and the only life that doesn't break through a God who made not one mistake.

As long as God is in the mix, a holy life doesn't need a fix.

A LONG PLACE FOR A LONG TIME

In a crime show, victims are in the wrong place at the wrong time, but if you admit your faults and surrender to Jesus, then soon you will be in a LONG place for a LONG time.

A long place in the heavens' sky where you'll see Christ from way up high.

A long place where the sky is blue and Jesus Christ is awaiting you.

A long place where you will unite with all the saints if living right.

A long place where it's only days of blessing God in happy ways, and a long place with each award to everyone who serves the Lord.

Let Heaven become your destiny as a place for life longevity.

A MIND
IS THE LAST THING YOU WANT TO WASTE

Somewhere in the Bible, it said, "Let this mind be in you which is also in Christ Jesus." Now a college fund got it right; a mind is a terrible thing to waste because a mind is the LAST THING YOU WANT TO WASTE.

The very last thing that you want to do is to waste a mind that's given to you. The very last thing that you want to lose is the mind of God you are meant to use. The very last thing that I want to think about is how life itself begins to stink.

The very last thing that should be taught is to think the actions that get you caught, and the only thing that you really need is the mind of Christ, and you shall succeed. That only happens when you find a place to use the mind that you cannot waste. Holla!!

A PART OF THE TEST

Somewhere in the Bible, Jesus was tempted by Satan in the wilderness. Like Jesus, you too had to endure temptation because it was part of the test to win God's best.

A part of the test that made you think how to keep your life from a hellish sink. A part of the test that gave us tears from the issues of life for many years. A part of the test that we had to take to see what choices we would make.

A part of the test that you couldn't ignore to see what God will have in store, and a part of the test that is here to stay 'cause you will be tempted every night and day. The Devil will flee if you just resist, and your name will be on Heaven's list. Peace out!!

A SAVE FROM THE GRAVE

I heard about a pastor's son who had a gunshot wound to the chest. Rushed to the hospital, it seemed he was going to die, but God kept and ordained him to be a youth and young adult pastor. Like the pastor's son, you too can tell how God made a SAVE from the GRAVE.

He made a save from a tragedy that could've killed both you and me.

He made a save from all the Hell you would have faced for how you fell.

He made a save from all the crimes you would have done so many times.

He made a save from each mistake you would have made for the Devil's sake, and he made a save from any loss when Jesus died on that rugged cross. So give him praise for a needed save that God has made from every grave.

A SINLESS WHISPER

Back in the 80s, I heard a song called "Careless Whisper." In the song, the singer refuses to dance because he cheated on his true love. But with Jesus, you can always dance no matter what you've done because Jesus Christ has a SINLESS whisper.

A kind of whisper that speaks so loud that it shuts the voices of a worldly crowd.

A kind of whisper that doesn't rush to tell your storm to be still and hush. A kind of whisper that wants your ears to listen to God, who calms your fears.

A kind of whisper that kills your pride if you take the Lord to be your guide, and a kind of whisper that makes you dance when you just receive a second chance.

Through the word of God, you can concur that Jesus Christ is your whisper. God bless y'all.

A SOARING LION

There was a song called Jesus the Lion of Judah when the enemy comes like a roaring lion, count on Jesus as a SOARING lion.

A soaring lion who will compete against the enemy's jaws of defeat.

A soaring lion who will stand and fight for the Lord's people each day and night.

A soaring lion who will protect all humankind from each regret.

A soaring lion who is everywhere to comfort you with love and care, and a soaring lion who will return to confront a world with no concern.

Pretty soon, there'll be no more dyin' for JESUS is our soaring lion.

A STAR FOR YOUR SCAR

While being crucified, Jesus had nails on his hands and nails on his feet. For enduring the cross, Jesus got rewarded when he rose from the dead. Like Jesus, you, too, must endure hardships, and by doing so, you'll receive a STAR for your scar.

A morning star for every pain from past defeats with the strength to gain.

A morning star for each regret that kept you in the Devil's net.

A morning star for every loss for a line you wished you'd never crossed.

A morning star for every fight you had within each day and night, and a morning star for all the tears you have cried throughout the years.

So offer praise to your morning star for blessing you through every scar.

A TRUTH OPERATOR

Back in the 80s, there was a song about a smooth operator who does things in big places. Back in the Bible, a man named Jesus Christ did things in all places, so like the singer wanted a smooth operator, you should want a TRUTH operator.

An operator you can call on how to shake it off like the Apostle Paul.

An operator who sees your pain which causes life to be insane.

An operator who knows for sure how to heal your body with every cure.

An operator who can truly see how to restore your heart without surgery.

An operator, unlike man, can see the damage without a scan, and an operator who once was dead can raise you from your dying bed.

So make an appointment with an operator in Jesus Christ sent by your creator.

A WIN IS NOT A WIN

Somewhere in the Bible, God says that the battle is not ours but belongs to him. If you choose to take matters into your own hands, then unlike sports, a win is NOT a win. It's not a win when you choose to fight without the Holy Ghost and all his might.

It's not a win when you think you're bad by doing what makes Jesus mad. It's not a win when you refuse to hear a God who doesn't lose.

It's not a win when you ignore what the word of God is looking for, and it's not a win when you make a choice not to obey your father's voice. Without the blessed trinity, you can win and lose simultaneously. God bless y'all.

ADDITION WITHOUT TRADITION

Somewhere in the Bible, the Pharisees believed in washing their hands before eating, yet their tradition dishonored their parents and violated God's word. This is a clear reminder of how you need the addition without tradition.

A true addition to your daily life like a husband is to his lovely wife.

A true addition to another day like a potter is to his molded clay.

A true addition to a peaceful night and a kind of future that's very bright.

A true addition to every choice that only pleases your savior's voice and a true addition that is spirit-led without tradition that thinks he's dead.

Why need tradition like the Pharisees when you can add Jesus Christ with ease?

AIN'T NO PROBLEM BIG ENOUGH

Back in the 60s, there was a song that said "Ain't no mountain high enough, ain't no valley low enough, and ain't no rhythm wide enough to keep me from getting to you." That is what God feels about you. No matter what you're facing, there ain't no problem big enough for your heavenly father.

There's not a problem that he cannot fix against the enemy and his worldly tricks.

There's not a problem that he wouldn't solve nor a miracle he couldn't involve.

There's not a problem that is way too big nor dirt in your life he cannot dig.

There's no problem that is way too great for the Lord your God to eliminate, and there's never a problem in society that can stop your God entirely.

So don't be fooled by the Devil's bluff 'cause there's nothing he does that is big enough. Peace out!!

AIN'T NOBODY BUSY ENOUGH

Back in the '60s, a song reminded us that ain't no mountain high enough nor a valley low enough for any duet. The same applies to all of us; there ain't nobody busy enough to spend time with God.

Not busy enough to meditate on how the Lord your God has been so great.

Not busy enough to relax and chill, you'll find yourself in Jehovah's will.

Not busy enough to settle down and give the Lord his kingdom crown.

Not busy enough to just read a verse that the Lord will use to break a curse, and not busy enough just to see for sure if Jesus thinks that you are mature. If he does not you must repent for a time with God that wasn't spent. Holla!!

ALL YOUR LIFE YOU HAD TO FIGHT

In the film, The Color Purple, Sofia angrily looks at Celie and says, "All my life, I had to fight." Like Sofia, you too can look over your life and explain how all YOUR life YOU had to fight.

How all your life you fought tooth and nail with the help of God who just cannot fail. How all your life you had to scratch and bite when seeking God with all your might. How all your life you fasted and prayed like Jesus did while being slayed.

How all your life you supposed to die but by God's grace you can testify, and how all your life you went through years of fighting demons and facing fears. Those trying years were worth the fight 'cause it gave you Christ as your only light. Peace out!!

ALMOST DOES COUNT

Over the years, you heard the saying, "Almost doesn't count." That may be true physically, but spiritually God has proven that almost DOES count through those who serve him.

Almost counts when looking back at how God saved you from any lack.

Almost counts when you think about how God kept you from any drought.

Almost counts when you take a look at how you're taken off the Devil's hook.

Almost counts when you take a pause and thank the Lord that he broke your walls, and almost counts when Jesus saved every one of you from the Devil's grave.

So praise the Lord who is on your side for coming to where you almost died.

AMERICA'S LESS WANTED

Back in the '80s, there was a crime show entitled America's Most Wanted. The purpose of the show was to get criminals off the streets and to the prison walls. Today America has done the same with God, removing the phrase "One nation under God."

Taking God off of schools has made him America's LESS wanted. He is less wanted when America makes it tender to marry your gender. He is less wanted when people turn to a national government, not an eternal covenant. He is less wanted when America calls it a shame to say Jesus' name, and God is less wanted when what he calls a sin has been viewed as a win.

The Bible says, "The wicked will turn into hell and all nations that forget God." This is your warning America, either you return to God or feel the WRATH of God.

AN IMMORTAL COMEBACK

Back in the 90s, a video game called Mortal Kombat where the fighters from Earth and another realm collided. Jesus had his Mortal Kombat when he died on an old rugged cross. It seemed that death had a victory until Jesus made AN IMMORTAL COMEBACK.

A type of comeback reaching deep inside to have victory over sin and pride.

A type of comeback refusing to die because it serves a God who just cannot lie.

A type of comeback going step by step against a defeat that it won't accept.

A type of comeback fighting every foe and telling Satan that he has to go, and a type of comeback that helps you thrive just like Jesus Christ, who's forever alive.

This immortal comeback is not a game but living proof that you're not the same. Peace out!!

AN OPEN DOOR TO THE POOR

Somewhere in the Bible, Jesus preached the gospel to the poor. Like Jesus, you, too, have been anointed to open the door to the poor.

To the very poor with none to eat, just give them food like bread and meat.

To the very poor who have no place, just give them Jesus and his saving grace.

To the very poor who's been denied, just show 'em love that Christ supplied.

To the very poor with none to drink, just give them water from Heaven's sink, and to the poor who are lost in sin please save their lives through Christ within.

That is what the love of God is just using his word to bless the poor.

ARE YOU CLEAR TO HEAR?

If you were to define prayer, it would be a conversation between you and God, but prayer isn't just talking to God but also listening to God. So before you go to Him in prayer, the Lord wants to know, "Are you clear to hear"?

Are you clear enough not to make a sound and just hear a God turning things around?

Are you clear enough not to ask a thing and just hear the voice of the risen king?

Are you clear enough not to ask for stuff and just hear from God when life is rough?

Are you clear enough to take a look at God's point of view in his living book, and are you very clear that before you speak, you will thank the Lord every single week?

If you say yes and there's evidence, you'll prevail in God's defense.

ARE YOU IN GOD'S HANDS?

Many years ago, a commercial came out with one question, are you in good hands? That is what the Lord's been asking, and today he wants to know, "Are you in GOD'S hands"?

Those holy hands of a risen king who is more worthy than golden bling? Those holy hands of the prince of peace who will sit with you at any feast? Those holy hands that you can trust as long you do not fall in lust?

Those holy hands you're gonna need for the hungry people you want to feed, and the only hands that protect you from the enemy and his evil crew. If you are not in the Lord's hands, you will end up on sinking sands. Peace out!!

ARE YOU IN THAT BOOK?

Somewhere in the Bible, those who aren't in the book of life will be cast into the lake of fire. So as you continue your daily walk, I just want to ask, "Are you in that book"?

Are you in the book that has given you every word from God you can look into?

Are you in the book with the evidence of miracles not making sense?

Are you in the book warning every town that the wrath of God is coming down?

Are you in the book that will end your day with hope from God if you just obey, and are you in the book that'll save your soul if you ask the Lord to take full control?

By saying yes, you are ready to fly and see the Lord reaching from the sky.

.

ARE YOU THAT WORD?

The Bible said in the beginning that the word was with God and became God. Someone needs a word for their situation, and today the Lord wants to know, "Are you that WORD"?

Are you the word from eternity for a world full of uncertainty?

Are you the word from the upper sky that tells someone they don't have to die?

Are you the word that has in store the food and water for the poor?

Are you the word that has in mind all hurting souls being left behind, and are you the word from God alone for those who thought they were on their own?

If that's a yes, you'll be going far as a living word that you really are.

AREN'T YOU FORGETTING?

Somewhere in the Bible, Paul forgets the things behind him, reaching forth the things before him. So anytime people bring up your past, you have to ask them, "Aren't you forgetting"?

Forgetting the fact that I'm not the same nor do I have the time for your silly game? Forgetting the fact that I'm moving on and who I was is now dead and gone? Forgetting that fact that you're just a fake who was using me for your own sake?

Forgetting the way you have offended me by keeping me in my history, and forgetting the fact that I have a friend in Jesus Christ whom I can depend. So go ahead and get upset, for, with Jesus Christ, I can now forget. Holla!!

ARE YOU A PHONY OR A TESTIMONY?

In our church today, there are Christians who are sometimes real and sometimes fake. With that being said, are you a PHONY or a TESTIMONY?

Are you a phony who would pretend to praise the Lord when you're not his friend?

Are you a phony who just decides to come to church after someone dies?

Are you a phony who only came 'cause it's Sunday morning in Jesus' name?

Are you a phony who's giving praise because you've got another raise, and are you a phony with little space for Jesus Christ and his loving grace?

If that's the case, you will live less until you break your phoniness.

ARE YOU CAREFUL TO THE CARELESS?

Too many people are stressed out because they've blessed the wrong things and wrong people. This leads me to one question, are you CAREFUL to the CARELESS?

Are you giving care to all of those who are dragging you to their living woes?

Are you giving care to all the stuff from everyone who's bad enough?

Are you giving care for all the crap from those who are in the Devil's trap?

Are you giving caring for all the junk from those who treat you like a punk?

Are you giving care to the very broke who is viewing life as a total joke, and are you giving care to the very lost, who refuse to bow to a greater boss?

If that's the case, you will keep the stress by helping those who could care less.

ARE YOU MAKING GOD SICK?

The church today has inconsistent believers, which leads me to ask, "Are you making God SICK"?

Are you making God want to spew you out just because you live in faith and doubt?

Are you making God want to take away his promises from you today?

Are you making God so very ill that he's cutting you out of his will?

Are you making God so sick to death by the filthy words from your breath, and are you making God want to go to bed 'cause you're mad at folks who now are dead?

If that's the case, the Lord will tick and use his wrath to make you sick.

A SIP OF WORSHIP

To receive living water, all it takes is a SIP of worship.

A living sip of honoring who Jesus is as risen king.

A living sip of bowing down and giving God his holy crown.

A living sip that meditates on God who rules the United States.

A living sip that determines to pardon you from all your sins, and a living sip that interacts with a living God who has all the facts.

So thank the Lord through every sip as a living proof of true worship.

BEEN THERE FELT THAT

While being crucified, Jesus, in agony, asked, "My God my God, why thou art has forsaken me"? At some point, we asked the Lord the same question, which is why Jesus wants to tell you that he's been there and felt that.

That pain he felt of being ignored by everyone whom he once adored.

That pain he felt of having lack from those he thought would have his back.

That pain he felt in the wilderness that he had to spend with the Devil's mess.

That pain he felt of being abused by those around him who seemed confused, and the pain he felt of having to die while his father sat from way up high.

Like each of you, Jesus Christ was there when life itself just didn't care.

A STAR FOR YOUR SCAR

While being crucified, Jesus had nails in his hands and nails in his feet; for enduring the cross, Jesus got rewarded when he rose from the dead. Like Jesus, you, too, must endure hardships; by doing so, you'll receive a STAR for your scar.

A morning star for every pain from past defeats with the strength to gain.

A morning star for each regret that kept you in the Devil's net.

A morning star for every loss for a line you wished you'd never crossed.

A morning star for every fight you had within each day and night, and a morning star for all the tears you have cried throughout the years.

So offer praise to your morning star for blessing you through every scar.

A START SURGERY

When a person has a heart attack, he or she undergoes heart surgery. The same is true for believers; when life gets hard, they must undergo a START surgery.

A surgery that will operate on those who have struggled as of late.

A surgery that will repair when life makes you wanna pull your hair.

A surgery that will replace any dying thoughts with the Lord's grace.

A surgery that will renew every person feeling sad and blue, and a surgery that motivates each one of us to see the Lord's face.

So ask the Lord for a surgery that will start a life for you and me.

A STRATEGY FOR TRAGEDY

In the Bible, Jesus waited four days to raise up Lazarus. Why would Jesus do that? Because, like his father, he had a STRATEGY for TRAGEDY.

A strategy that secretly revealed ways to be cancer-free.

A strategy that carefully removes doubts of the enemy.

A strategy so powerful it'll make you so unstoppable.

A strategy so dominant with miracles yet to be sent, and a strategy from way up high from a true God who will never die.

For those who face a tragedy, your living God has a strategy.

A JOY FRIEND

Before looking for a girlfriend or a boyfriend, you should consider a JOY friend.

A joy friend from eternity who is always there for you and me.

A joy friend from the upper sky who will never tell a single lie.

A joy friend from a trinity that will bless you so graciously.

A joy friend who is never late when he goes out for a single date, and a joy friend you'll want to spend your life with 'til the very end.

Today's the day to turn on the lights with a joy friend named Jesus Christ.

A WEB OF DEFEAT

In our society, there are people who have a web of deceit, that we came from the Devil, which will lead to a web of DEFEAT.

A kind of web where people lose by suffering each bump and bruise.

A kind of web where people fall 'cause they told the Lord they know it all.

A kind of web where people sink for all the times they failed to think.

A kind of web where people die by using drugs and getting high, and a kind of web where you will burn if you refuse to make the turn.

That needed turn from a total loss to Jesus Christ and his rugged cross.

A TOXIC FACE

Life will be a toxic waste if you choose to hold a toxic FACE.

A toxic face you had from years of getting folks in total tears.

A toxic face you held so long over everyone who did you wrong.

A toxic face that you have shown from the pain you felt that made you groan.

A toxic face that you have kept from a seed that God would not accept, and a toxic face you cannot hide from the bitterness toward the ones who died.

Until you lose that toxic face you will never see Jehovah's grace.

A YEARNING POINT

In life, you reach a turning point, but in Christ, you'll reach a YEARNING point.

A point of yearning for the Lord through eternal life as my reward.

A point of yearning for a king who gave the church a song to sing.

A point of yearning for a time where Christ is more than any dime.

A point of yearning for a start that will give you a much cleaner heart, and a point of yearning for a grace that God will give at any place.

It's time to find your yearning point and be the one God will anoint.

ABOVE THE FLAW

Above the flaw of every choice, you've made to please the Devil's voice.

Above the flaw of every thought that would cause you to feel distraught.

Above the flaw of what you've done that kept you from the begotten son.

Above the flaw of what you've said toward everyone with the living bread, and above the flaw of who you were that made your life a total blur.

You may never be above the law, but with Christ, you are above the FLAW.

ALL YOU CAN DO IS PRAY

In a chaotic society, all you can do is PRAY.

All you can do is shut the door and ask the Lord to do even more.

All you can do is shut the light on anything that isn't right.

All you can do is shut the fear and make your prayers loud and clear.

All you can do is put your trust in a God who sees each one of us, and all you can do is put your mind on a God who's never hard to find.

He'll be with you throughout the day if you just decide to fast and pray.

ARE YOU CARELESS ABOUT THE CAREFUL?

In our struggles, we've asked God to help us, and he did. Today people love the blessing more than the blesser, which makes me wonder, "Are you CARELESS about the CAREFUL?"

Are you caring less about everyone who's connected to the begotten son?

Are you caring less about everything that's connected to our risen king?

Are you caring less about families who were struggling like the least of these?

Are you caring less about giving back to all those who suffer lack, and are you caring less about giving hope to lives that have reached the final rope?

If that's the case, you are in a mess without knowing it for caring less.

ARE YOU LOSING YOUR HAIR?

I've heard in the Bible that Samson found strength through his hair. Life has ways of making us weak which leads me to wonder, "Are you losing your HAIR"?

Are you losing your hair due to the total stress of facing those who could care less?

Are you losing your hair due to a total lack of finding those who would give back?

Are you losing your hair due to constant fear that judgment day is coming near?

Are you losing your hair due to the constant ways your life in Christ could face delays?

Are you losing your hair 'cause the bills are due, and there's not enough money in store for you, and are you losing your hair 'cause the enemy is attacking you internally?

If that's a yes, your God is there to give you the strength to regrow your hair.

ARE YOU THAT ONE?

In the Bible, Jesus healed ten lepers, but only one came back to give thanks. As you reflect on where you were, I just want to know, "Are you that ONE?"

That one believer of Jesus Christ who now can see his holy lights?

That one believer of God alone whom you know for sure can set the tone?

That one believer of happiness as a key to having your father's rest?

That one believer of life ahead who gives daily praise to the living bread, and that one believer of life up there who is thanking God for his love and care?

If you're that one, you are on your way to a better life until the Lord's day.

ARE YOU THERE YET?

Remember when children ask, "are we there yet?". Well today, God is asking, "Are YOU there yet"?

Are you yet there in your proper place to give the Lord his rightful space?

Are you yet there in your proper role of asking God to make you whole?

Are you yet there in your proper spot of giving Christ a daily shot?

Are you yet there in your proper room where you're the bride and Christ the groom and are you yet there in this present day to listen to what God would say?

If you have not, then get to where you will be blessed for being there.

AREN'T YOU THANKFUL
FOR WHAT YOU'RE NOT?

Now that Jesus saved you, aren't you thankful for what you're not?

That you are not another soul who puts himself in Satan's hole?

That you are not another man who's killing with a bloody hand?

That you are not the same old jerk who's cursing folks while you're at work?

That you are not the same old punk abusing folks and talking junk, and that you're not what people say but whom God sees each and every day?

Give the Lord a daily spot by thanking him for what you're not.

BE WATER MY CHILD

Martial arts great Bruce Lee once said that water in a cup becomes a cup, water in a bottle becomes a bottle, and water in a teapot becomes a teapot. He also mentioned that water could flow or crash. He ended his point by saying, "Be water, my friend."

Isn't that what God is saying? If so, then it's time to hear that voice saying, "Be water my child".

That living water to someone's hurt that will forgive everybody's dirt.

That living water to someone's pain through the lamb of God, who was fully slain.

That living water for someone's cry to a holy God who cannot lie.

That living water that calms the mind when life itself has you deaf and blind, and the living water of the Holy Ghost will guide someone as their only host. You'll be amazed at how people grow when having you as their H20. BE WATER MY CHILD.

BE WATER MY LORD

Martial artist Bruce Lee once said that water in a cup becomes a cup, water in a bottle becomes a bottle, and water in a teapot becomes a teapot. He added that water could either flow or crash. He ended his point with the words, "Be water, my friend."

Would you like to say that to the Lord? Then all you have to do is go before him and say, "Be water, my Lord."

That spiritual water that cleanses me from the years of guilt and calamity.

That spiritual water that renews my soul through the love of Jesus that makes me whole.

That spiritual water that forgives my faults and keeps me free from the Devil's cults.

That spiritual water that showers us with the word of God against worldly lust, and the spiritual water that I'm gonna take to pardon someone for each mistake.

So be the water that will purify so that no one else will have to die. Peace out!!

BE YOUR OWN BEST FRIEND

Friendship is one of the best things in life, but what if you don't have any friends? Well, you can have self-pity or the courage to be your own BEST FRIEND.

Be your own friend, so you can find a way to have some peace of mind.

Be your own friend, so you can make who you really are a piece of cake.

Be your own friend, so you can see how to live your life so happily.

Be your own friend so you can do what God has put inside of you, and be your own friend so you can stay with Jesus Christ each night and day.

In doing so, you won't depend on anyone to be your friend.

A THRILL TO KILL

People who kill aren't people; they are MONSTERS full of lust, greed, and control. And since the law means nothing, they'll do anything to anyone 'cause there's a society that just has a THRILL to KILL.

A total thrill for every knife they're gonna use to take a life.

A total thrill for every gun they plan to use to kill someone.

A total thrill for every plan to cause the death of any man.

A total thrill to see the pain of all victims who have been slain, and a total thrill to see the dead in a pool of blood that's colored red.

No human being will have the thrill of psychopaths who love to kill.

BE THE LIGHT WHEN THE TIME IS RIGHT

The Bible makes it clear that Jesus is the light of the world. Our world has become a very dark place, and God wants you to be the LIGHT when the time is RIGHT.

Become the light when the world is dark that's willing to give that needed spark.

Become the light when the world is dim, spreading God's love that's never slim.

Become the light that's gonna shine when someone's life isn't doing fine.

Become the light that's gonna bring every lost soul to the mighty king, and become the light that won't go out and shows what Christ is all about.

He's all about just living right by obeying God and being the light.

AS IF GOD IS PRAYING TO YOU

With the world under attack, you must live as if God is praying to you.

As if the Lord is on his knees and speaking to all families.

As if the Lord is on his hands by touching souls in all the lands.

As if the Lord is on his feet, just waiting for his mercy seat.

As if the Lord is looking up to those who gonna fill his cup.

As if the Lord is looking straight to those who help him elevate, and as if the Lord is looking for a group of saints to help the poor.

The time is now to live a day like the Holy Ghost will fast and pray.

ARE YOU KILLING YOURSELF?

Not all suicides are intentional, which leads to one question, are you KILLING yourself?

Are you killing yourself by telling lies on every person who's on the rise?

Are you killing yourself by telling jokes that ain't so funny to other folks?

Are you killing yourself by talking smack about everyone while smoking crack?

Are you killing yourself by talking crap that's keeping in the devil's trap?

Are you killing yourself by doing stuff that placed someone on each handcuff, and are you killing yourself every day and night by getting into a silly fight?

If that's the case, then you better chill before your inner man gets overkill.

ARE YOU COMING TO CHRIST?

The Bible said, "let us go to the house of the Lord." But everyone who goes isn't there for Jesus. So instead of coming to church, the real question is are you coming to CHRIST?

Are you coming to Christ who really knows how to go through life's most vicious blows?

Are you coming to Christ who really sees that humankind ain't worth to please?

Are you coming to Christ who really hears the weeping sounds of your own tears?

Are you coming to Christ who is always there to save his people everywhere, and are you coming to Christ who will set you free once you give your life to eternity?

If you are not, you will be dead unless you come to the living bread.

A PROMISED STAND

To get to the promise land, you must first take a promised STAND.

A promised stand for righteousness to bless the ones who've been given less.

A promised stand for righteous things like eternal life from the King of Kings.

A promised stand for a mom and dad to save their child from a world so mad.

A promised stand for the Holy Ghost to bless someone, who needs God the most, and a promised stand through the rugged cross to save someone from every loss.

The more you take a promised stand, the better you'll go to a higher land.

A HOLY GHOST SHOWER

If you want the Holy Ghost power, you must first take a Holy Ghost SHOWER.

A holy shower that makes you clean from a world today that's dark and mean.

A holy shower that makes you sweat through a loving grace that you won't forget.

A holy shower that purifies a dirty world from Satan's lies.

A holy shower that's sending down a word from God to every town, and a holy shower you'll always need to resist the thoughts of lust and greed.

Spend time with God for at least an hour, and you'll be cleansed in a holy shower.

A ROAD TO THE FINAL DOOR

In college basketball, there is the "Road to the Final Four," but in life, there is a road to the final DOOR.

The final door is where you'll be if serving God consistently.

The final door is where you'll go for every seed you plan to sow.

The final door is your reward for all the souls you have restored.

The final door is your retreat for saving souls from sure defeat, and the final door will let you in if you do confess every filthy sin.

Once you do then you're gonna soar to Heaven with the final door.

ABOUT THE AUTHOR

Born in Los Angeles, California, Jason E. White learned to write at an early age. After high school, he attended Santa Monica College and studied English. It was through writing essays that Jason found his passion for poetry.

In his spare time, Jason volunteers at Good Samaritan Hospital, and in 2021, he was named the hospital's Volunteer of the Year. His purpose is to use his writing to teach, uplift, and encourage people.

www.ingramcontent.com/pod-product-compliance
Lightning Source LLC
Chambersburg PA
CBHW051543120626
46551CB00013B/1350